Move Over, Rover!

Starting a doggy daycare business from home using a popular online pet sitting service.

INTRODUCTION:

I'm about to take you from being a good person with an earnest desire to make extra money with a love of dogs and turn you into a successful entrepreneur.

The information you learn in this guide is based on my already tested and successful model of online marketing combined with other methods I have tested in person and still use to this day. Everything I recommend in this guide is something I've tried and tested myself. I'm going to give you some solid ideas that will absolutely work in this market and will further spark great ideas of your own.

Basically, this guide will help you succeed. But I cannot force you to do the recommended action steps. I cannot make you take action on all the information. That is up to you.

Some people may feel nervous or anxious along the way, or overwhelmed if some of the steps recommended are new to them and unfamiliar to their comfort zones.

This is normal. However, this guide shows you how to accomplish the mission whether you do the steps or you pay someone else a tiny fee to do them for you. How great is that?

It's fail-proof. I became an entrepreneur out of necessity myself. I hate having a boss monitor my activities. I value my freedom and free time. I like helping people and solving problems without playing office politics or kissing up to the boss.

Asking "how can I help people and who needs help?" is almost always the path to money. Money's a good thing and I'm going to show you how to help more people and how to make more money.

So do the work, there's not much work involved if you'll just get it done and over with and don't look back.

1. Get In the Game Immediately

Rover.com is like UBER, the business where you sign up as a driver with your car and they send you customers. Rover.com can get you customers to start out with for starting your doggy boarding or daycare from home business.

The reality is most people suck at customer service, that also means many if not most existing Rover sitters. This is a great opportunity for any Rover sitter to shine, like *you* and you'll be a Rover sitter by the end of this chapter.

Many if not most existing "professional" doggy daycares in town are staffed by rude employees and suck just like the Rover sitters, which is why Rover.com is so successful in getting their customers too. So you have a giant opportunity to carve out a smooth and successful money making doggy loving customer helping operation by relying on the fact that most existing doggy day care is about average, nothing spectacular usually.

I say this out of complete honesty as a traveler who's been all around the Western US and seen some of the best and worst doggy day care, dog parks, and areas of extreme opportunity for anyone wanting to get in on the doggy boarding game from home, even if it's to have enough extra money a month for a new car or to go clothes shopping without worrying about hurting the budget.

If you make "mistakes" however while undertaking your Rover.com doggy boarding duties that get you flagged with Rover, then your customer base can and will dry up overnight. Your listing will likely be moved down or completely removed from the search queue for potential customers on Rover.com without any warning. I prepare you for this possibility and how to overcome it or avoid it entirely.

With our web and flyer strategy, we'll be protecting and hedging against this unlikely, but possible, rainy day scenario while expanding your customer and income base.

1st action step: <u>Go right now and sign up as a sitter on Rover.com</u> and complete your profile, this will get you in the game immediately

1. SIGN UP TO BECOME A SITTER WITH ROVER.COM

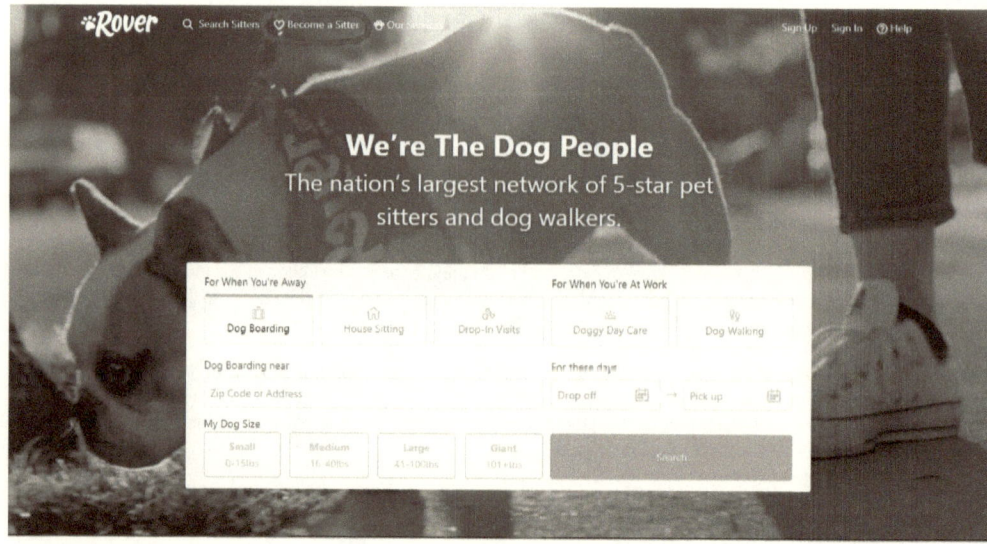

2. **BONUS**: SIGN UP WITH WAG! DOG WALKING SERVICE

EVERYTHING YOU NEED TO KNOW ABOUT ROVER.COM

Rover.com is a trusted online community where dog owners can connect with loving and trustworthy dog lovers to have them watch their dogs while they're away. You can expect to make anywhere from $20 – 50 per night sitting a dog.

Or as a consumer, you can find a dog sitter just about anywhere while you're travelling or even in your own zip code. Just search using their website or app. Rover.com is the nation's largest network of pet lovers for hire, with more than 50,000 pet sitters and dog walkers across the country who are easily accessible online. Dog sitting fees are listed up-front as well as the services offered along with the kind of animals the pet sitter is comfortable with.

What services do they offer and I can make money from?

Rover.com offers a host of services including dog hosting, dog sitting, and dog walking.

While dog boarding is the main service they offer, they also offer pet care for other animals like cats and birds. Plus, Rover has a 24-hour vet service, so a certified veterinarian is always a phone call away if your pet falls sick while you are away, or if you, the sitter are wondering how to handle a bad situation with a sick or injured animal.

The company also has a mobile app, at no cost. The app makes communication between sitters and pet parents easy and great for travelers who just arrived in town and need to unload Fido before checking into a hotel.

Can you make money sitting dogs from home?

A short answer to this question is, yes. *Dog sitting is one of the easiest ways to make extra money from home.* If you have been wondering where to get dog-sitting jobs, Rover.com is quite possibly your best option for starting and getting a feel for running your own independent operation.

As a sitter booking through Rover, you are an independent contractor, meaning you decide whether or not you wish to sit dogs part-time, full-time, provide doggy daycare, or overnight and you set your daily rate. Also, as an independent contractor or home business owner, you may be entitled to a tax exemption for dog boarding in your house.

(When its tax filing time, Google "exemptions and deductions for home business use" to see if you can qualify, there's a good chance you do)

However, to be on the safe side and maximize your earnings, you will also likely want to get business outside of Rover.com and not become completely dependent upon them in the event that you get a bad review and they decide to move you down the list of available sitters. I know people that this has happened to, and I explain all about how to overcome this challenge in this guide, which will save you time, headaches and heartbreak.

No one likes it when the money dries up all of a sudden. It's a bad day for a business owner.

How much can you make per day running your own doggy daycare or boarding business?

The amount of money you can make through dog boarding with rover.com and in conjunction with your own website (which I'm going to show you how to set up in only 10 minutes) is dependent on the number of days you are available, how often you sit and the kind of dogs you sit. Realize that dogs with medical issues usually command a higher rate.

If you are an enthusiastic sitter, making $1000 per month is entirely possible. That's a lot of money towards buying a new car, saving for a big purchase or saving for your next holiday or vacation. Set your rates and you sit as much or as little as you want; so it's up to you.

A key tip is do not under price your services, or else you will attract cheapskates and lower quality clients. Do not attempt to appeal to all people. Find your best clients and set your price to attract the right clients. This will take time and some adjustments as you observe the clients you get. Remember, you're still doing people a huge service and helping them, so it's still kinda work and everyone should be paid fairly for exceptional service.

According to research, more than 43 million homes own pets in the US. Those households are not with their pets 24/7 though. Therefore, Rover.com makes it easier for these households to find pet sitters to take care of their dogs while they are away, as well as create a substantial supplemental or full-time income leveraging their house and yard or free time. Some sitters can even sit dogs in the owner's home, more on this later.

2. TIPS TO START A SUCCESSFUL DOG BOARDING BUSINESS

Dog daycare and boarding/sitting businesses are growing in popularity these days. This leaves an opportunity for people who love pets to make money off this trend by starting their own dog day care businesses.

Rover.com has made it possible for pet lovers to make an extra few hundred dollars each month easily by sitting dogs through the platform right away with little experience, but you'll need some basics in dog handling to get started on the proper foot.

Below are vital tips and information about
dogs for new dog sitters.

- **Dog behavior**

Each dog has a unique presence and personality. Some are timid or shy around strangers while others are super-playful and willing to play with other dogs or with the sitter. Some dogs don't get along well with other dogs.

So before you board a dog, be sure to ask the dog owner about the dog's behaviors if that makes you feel more comfortable, but don't be rude or intrusive about it. The behaviors of the dog must be considered carefully before deciding to sit the dog. Also, ask whether the dog has any medical issue. Dogs with medical problems typically command a higher rate as they are hard to handle.

- **Safety handling**

Perhaps you sense when people want some personal space or would not interact with others. Well, dogs have similar feelings and these pets, like humans, need their boundaries to be respected if the relationship is to go beyond the first meeting.

You have to learn how to stop a dog when it is misbehaving. I find using a strong commanding voice and being willing to tap a dog on the nose is often times enough.

- **Dog aggression**

Most dog owners won't admit that their dog is aggressive or violent. The truth is certain breeds are more aggressive and violent. Dog breeds that have been portrayed as aggressive include German shepherds, bloodhounds, pit bulls, huskies and Doberman pinschers.

Before you take up the task, be sure to meet the owner and the dog to get a feel for the dog. If it's not a good fit just say you need some time to think it over, and then get back to them with your decision later.

- **Dog feeding**

Dogs can be allergic to almost any food ingredient. Nonetheless, there are certain foods that are likely to trigger an allergic reaction in dogs. If the dog is allergic to certain foods or is on a special diet, then it's best to give the pet her regular food.

*Never feed a dog chocolate, it's deadly.

*Keep some dog food on hand but expect the dog owner to bring the dog's food for overnight stays.

Also, it's a good idea to feed dogs separately and privately so they don't fight over the food. Remember, strange dogs may attack each other competing for food. This is something you want to avoid for your own safety and the safety of every dog in your custody.

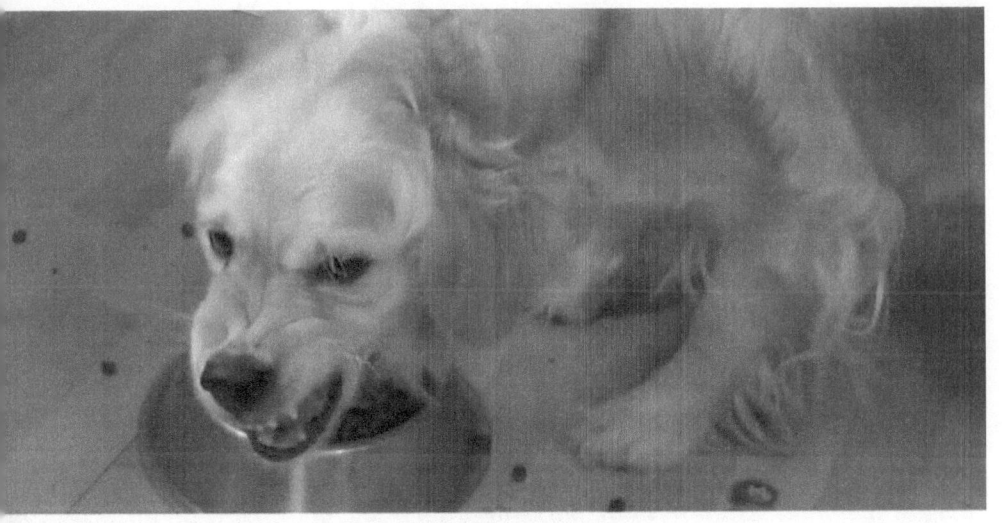

Imagine having to tell a dog owner their dog was killed because another dog went crazy on it during a feeding frenzy.

- **What are the pros and cons of all this doggy business?**

Starting a doggy daycare business can be a lucrative as well as emotionally fulfilling career choice for dog lovers. The best thing about this venture is that you don't need any training or special experience.

You only have to love pets and know how to take good care of them. Also, there are no significant start-up fees. The business is not without challenges though. The main challenge is that you must be very responsible and accountable. You need to be patient and comfortable handling potential and rare animal emergencies.

The real upsides to doing doggy boarding from home is that you can make some money and build a business at the same time. With extra money comes more freedom, and for the most part you're just hanging around 3 or 4 dogs all day. If you're charging $30 a night and you watch 3 dogs a night only 2 days a week, that's a potential $720 extra income for relatively easy and dare I say fun work with no boss breathing down your neck.

The downsides of having a doggy daycare business are having to schedule pickup/dropoff times with clients, having a guest dog in your house pee or poop on the floor or furniture, losing one of your favorite blankets to a chew toy, having a dog bite you, having a dog get sick or die in your custody (rare but not impossible).

Action step: to get a better understanding of dogs, Google "dog park <name of your town>" and visit a few dog parks to observe the dogs. How and why do you think the dogs are separated into small and large? Why do most dog parks list as a rule not to bring food in? Which dogs are playing and which are being aggressive to dominate and harm other dogs?

- **Conclusion:**

Once you have your first pet boarding job and bond with the dog involved, you will realize that you have just found a great and fun way to make money doing something you love. Then when you actually get paid, you'll feel the joy of self-employment and self-sufficient income.

You may not want to run a doggy boarding business for the rest of your life. That's quite alright. You'll always have something you can fall back on with this or to supplement your income in the future as you wish.

Also, running any business gives you incredibly valuable business experience and insight which you can apply towards new businesses. Once you get the entrepreneurial spirit, a world of potential solutions opens to you just waiting to be found. This is the basis of the free market and potentially getting rich. Most people who get rich create something useful and it helps a lot of people. Simple but not easy.

Either you're okay with being an employee or a worker, or you have a desire to be your own boss. There's no judgment regardless of your decision, but I hate having a boss judging everything I do all day. Just not what I like in life personally.

3. GETTING YOUR DOGGY BUSINESS OFF THE GROUND RIGHT

I. Consult local authorities beforehand; know the laws.

Some residential areas are no pet zones or restrict certain kind of business activities. It is therefore imperative to know the laws before starting this kind of business. If it is legal, you may require obtaining certain licenses in order to be allowed to operate.

However, to be completely honest, as long as you keep enough of a low profile there's no reason why anyone should ever know you're running a dog boarding business from home. Don't be super flashy or tell everyone on your block about it they may not appreciate it.

II. Be considerate to your neighbors

A pack of dogs in your backyard is not a group of pious monks on meditation They are bound to be noisy and mischievous and sometimes even rough. This is why it's so important to screen your dog clients to select the best behaved dogs for regular sitting to avoid problems in the noise pollution and/or chaos department.

If a neighbor asks, you can always say you're just watching dogs for some friends/co workers. If you have excess activity at your house, i.e. strange cars coming an going all the time, you can start to look like a drug dealer. Be considerate to your neighbors and do your operations wisely, and covertly to avoid suspicion or disturbing other people's home lives.

III. **Think Smart money. Start small, work up. Don't stress.**

Start off with 1 or 2 dogs, 3 or 4 at max. You should find a nice way to make a couple extra hundred bucks a week like this. Even people with huge yards and large houses will take no more than 8 – 9 dogs at a time. At that point you need more than 1 person to watch the dogs and you'll likely need pro grade boarding equipment like cages to be on the safe side.

This is why it's so important to *find your perfect balance* of the right dog clients, the right dogs, the right number of dogs, and the right amount of money to make and charge- to make everything worthwhile.

Separating dogs in the event it becomes necessary is as easy as putting them in separate rooms in your house if you choose. So long as all the dogs get together fine, they will likely want to sleep near or on top of each other all bunched up. You could also create stalls if you needed with some simple dividers or child gates, but with the right mix of dogs this won't be an issue.

Tip: Do NOT leave all the dogs together alone. Do not assume they'll all be fine if you step out for even 10 – 15 minutes. Dogs unsupervised can and will attack each other, and then you'll have a whole heapin' mess of problems to deal with.

IV.   **Benchmark with the best, get tips from the pros**

Visit doggy daycare and boarding services posing as a customer and learn best practices or ask for a tour of their facilities. Read their reviews online. It's usually quite simple though. Love the dogs, feed them, and ensure their safety.

V.   **Offer competitive and/or elite pricing**

Many business consultants advise starting at lower prices and gradually increasing the prices as the business becomes known. However, do no charge too low as it may lead to losses. Some customers might also think that your services are substandard.

People like me don't mind spending $35 a night for dog boarding if you're a super nice person who's easy going and keep a clean house with a yard where the vibe is good. I actually want to pay more for my doggy boarding because I want the person who treats my dog like a person or family member, not a number.

Conclusion

A home dog boarding business is easy to start and get off the ground as it is not necessarily capital intensive. It does not require much space and can be carried out in the backyard. You can charge an average of $ 20 to $25 per animal per day easily and if you keep the costs low, you can make a tidy sum of money without much effort or maintenance costs.

Action Step: Research the average, highest and lowest price for dog boarding and doggy daycare both on Rover.com for your city/area and consider them thoughtfully.... who has the most reviews? Who has the most positive reviews? Why is one person succeeding over another sitter? What do the best rover.com sitter profiles look like in your opinion and how can you apply it to your own?

4. THE ALTERNATIVE: HOW TO START A SUCCESSFUL DOG WALKING OR DOG SITTING (IN THEIR HOME) BUSINESS

SOME PEOPLE DON'T HAVE A HOUSE WITH MANY ROOMS OR A YARD. SOME PEOPLE MAY NOT EVEN HAVE AN APARTMENT. YOU MIGHT BE A COLLEGE STUDENT LIVING IN THE DORM AND CAN'T KEEP DOGS IN YOUR ROOM. THAT WOULDN'T STOP YOU FROM WALKING SOMEONE'S DOGS IN THE PARK OR SITTING SOMEONE'S DOG IN THEIR HOUSE FOR MONEY.

ACTUALLY, SITTING DOGS IN THE RICH FOLKS' HOMES IS WHAT YOU'D WANT TO BOTH ENJOY THEIR BIG HOUSES WHILE PLAYING WITH THEIR DOGS AND DOING YOUR HOMEWORK. BETTER THAN A HOTEL ROOM IN MANY REGARDS, KINDA FUN AND YOU CAN MAKE MONEY WHILE HOUSE SITTING TOO.

EXERCISE: WRITE DOWN A LIST OF 5 PLACES IN YOUR AREA WHERE THE AFFLUENT AND WEALTHY LIVE WHERE YOU COULD PUT UP A FLYER ADVERTISING THAT YOU ARE A RESPONSIBLE COLLEGE STUDENT/EXPERIENCED DOG HANDLER WHO CAN SIT THEIR DOGS WHILE THEY TRAVEL OR GO OUT ON THE TOWN... IS THERE A STARBUCKS OR A FITNESS CENTER IN A RICH PART OF TOWN WHERE YOU MIGHT KINDLY ASK OR JUST GO AHEAD AND PUT UP A FLYER ADVERTISING YOUR USEFUL SERVICE?

WALKING SOMEONE ELSE'S DOG IN THE PARK IS AN EASY WAY FOR YOU TO HELP A SENIOR OR PERSON WITH A DISABILITY WHO CAN'T EXERCISE THEIR DOG.

EXERCISE: GOOGLE DOG FRIENDLY ASSISTED LIVING CENTERS, DISABLED ORGANIZATIONS IN YOUR TOWN, OR THE LOCAL CHURCHES IN YOUR AREA THAT MIGHT BE INTERESTED IN HELPING YOU CONNECT WITH SENIORS AND THE DISABLED WHO HAVE DOGS, LOOK FOR VETERANS ORGANIZATIONS AS WELL

KEY TIP: DO NOT WALK 3 OR 4 DOGS AT THE SAME TIME. DO NOT USE THE PUBLIC DOG PARK AS YOUR FRONT OFFICE AND MAIN BASE OF OPERATIONS FOR DOG WALKING. YOU WILL STRESS YOURSELF OUT AND/OR POTENTIALLY CREATE A HAZARDOUS SITUATION AS WELL AS REDUCE THE ENJOYMENT OF REGULAR PEOPLE WHO ARE NOT RUNNING A DOG BUSINESS AND JUST WANT TO ENJOY SOME TIME AT THE PARK STRESS FREE.

6. FINDING CUSTOMERS WITH AND WITHOUT ROVER.COM

YOU COULD BE THE BEST PERSON TO BE AROUND DOGS, THE MOST RESPONSIBLE, AND HAVE THE BEST HOME AND HEART FOR DOGS, BUT IF YOU NEVER GET A CUSTOMER, THEN YOU ARE JUST TWIDDLING YOUR THUMBS AND NOT MAKING MONEY.

HERE IS A LIST OF CONCRETE THINGS YOU'LL NEED TO DO TO ENSURE THE FLOW OF CUSTOMERS. IF YOU DO NOT DO ALL THESE THINGS, THEN YOU ARE LEAVING MONEY ON THE TABLE AND YOU ARE NOT GIVING THIS ENTIRE ENDEAVOR THE 100% THAT IS POSSIBLE IN ORDER TO SUCCEED.

I AM NOT SAYING THAT YOU WON'T HAVE SUCCESS BY JUST USING ROVER.COM, BUT A WISE EXPRESSION I HAVE ALWAYS KEPT AS A PRIMARY BUSINESS OPERATING PRINCIPLE IS: "DON'T PUT ALL YOUR EGGS IN ONE BASKET". IN A DISPUTE WHO KNOWS IF ROVER.COM WILL TAKE YOUR SIDE OR THE CUSTOMER'S SIDE, AND IF IT TURNS OUT BAD FOR YOU, THEN YOU COULD LOSE ALL YOUR BUSINESS OVERNIGHT. I KNOW PEOPLE THIS HAS HAPPENED TO.

LET'S GET GOING HERE:

1. OPTIMIZE YOUR ROVER.COM SITE

YOU SHOULD INCLUDE HAPPY SMILING PICTURES OF YOU AND DOGS. PICTURES OF YOUR YARD AND YOUR CLEAN HOME SHOULD BE IN YOUR ROVER PROFILE. DO A SEARCH OF EXISTING ROVER SITTERS IN YOUR ZIP CODE TO SEE THE SITTERS WITH THE HIGHEST POSITIVE REVIEW RATINGS. NOTICE THE GOOD THINGS ABOUT THEIR PROFILES THAT WOULD MAKE YOU WANT TO SELECT THEM TO WATCH YOUR DOG IF YOU WERE A CUSTOMER.

2. GET YOUR WEBSITE UP LIKE RIGHT NOW (NOT OPTIONAL)

THIS STEP IS NOT OPTIONAL, IT IS SO INCREDIBLY IMPORTANT. WITHOUT THIS STEP, YOU ARE JUST REFUSING TO MAKE MORE MONEY THE EASY WAY.

THIS IS THE SINGLE MOST IMPORTANT STEP THAT EVERY ROVER.COM SITTER IS NOT DOING. IF YOU DO THIS, YOU WILL GAIN A TREMENDOUS ADVANTAGE OVER BOTH ROVER.COM SITTERS AND TRADITIONAL DOGGY DAYCARES EQUALLY. YOU WILL BE LIKE A FISHERMAN WITH 2 BOATS. BUT I AM GOING TO GIVE YOU A 3RD BOAT AS WELL JUST TO TOP IT OFF.

3. A SIMPLE FLIER CAMPAIGN TAKES 1 AFTERNOON AND CAN PAY OFF FOREVER

I GOT MY 1ST ONLINE MARKETING CLIENT WITH A FLIER. IT WILL BE MUCH EASIER TO GET DOGGY DAYCARE CLIENTS THAN ONLINE MARKETING CLIENTS WITH FLIERS IF YOU DO IT MY WAY.

THIS ALL SOUNDS LIKE IT COULD GET COMPLICATED, TECHNICAL, ARTISTIC, AND OVERWHELMING.

WRONG. YOU ARE GOING TO EITHER MAKE A SUPER SIMPLE WEBSITE THAT HITS ALL NECESSARY POINTS AND COME UP WITH A BASIC PHOTOCOPYABLE FLYER THAT HAS THE KEY POINTS OF INFORMATION (CAN BE HAND WRITTEN) YOURSELF, OR YOU'RE GOING TO GET SOMEONE ELSE TO MAKE IT FOR YOU FOR CHEAP ON FIVERR.COM, WHICH IS A WEBSITE WHERE YOU CAN GET SIMPLE THINGS LIKE WEBSITES AND FLIERS MADE FOR YOU INEXPENSIVELY.

SO THERE'S NO EXCUSE. IF YOU HAVE TO YOU WILL GIVE THESE FOLKS YOUR KEY INFO ABOUT YOUR DOGGY DAYCARE AND THEY'RE GOING TO

MAKE YOU THE ITEMS. YOU'LL HAVE TO SEARCH FIVERR.COM FOR THE SERVICES YOU NEED LIKE "BUILD ME A WEBSITE" OR "BUSINESS FLIERS".

IT ONLY HAS TO BE DONE RIGHT ONCE. ONCE YOU HAVE A SIMPLE FUNCTIONAL WEBSITE AND A FLIER DESIGN, YOU JUST USE IT OVER AND OVER AGAIN. THE CREATIVE WORK IS DONE.

IN THIS NEXT CHAPTER I'LL DISCUSS HOW TO DO IT STEP BY SIMPLE STEP.

7. 10 MINUTES TO INTERNET STARDOM

THE WEBSITE YOU'RE GOING TO MAKE IS SIMPLE. IF YOU WANT TO MAKE A SUPER FANCY WEBSITE, FEEL FREE. BUT I'M JUST GOING TO SPELL OUT WHAT YOU ABSOLUTELY NEED. AND YOU ABSOLUTELY NEED A WEBSITE. IF YOU ARE NOT GOING TO DO THIS STEP, YOU MIGHT AS WELL THROW MONEY IN THE TRASH CAN AND SET IT ON FIRE.

THE EASY WAY TO SETUP YOUR WEBSITE:

1.   GO TO GODADDY.COM

2.   REGISTER A NEW DOMAIN (A DOMAIN IS ALSO YOUR WEBSITE LIKE SAMSDOGSITTING.COM OR COMFYDOGSTAY.COM)

3.   GET HOSTING WITH GODADDY.COM

4.   SETUP YOUR WEBSITE EASIEST AND FASTEST BY INSTALLING WORDPRESS IN YOUR HOSTING ACCOUNT.

DON'T WORRY. WATCH THIS VIDEO. THIS VIDEO WILL EXPLAIN EVERYTHING YOU NEED. WATCH IT AND DO THE STEPS. WATCH IT NOW!!! DO THE STEPS NOW!!!!! THANK YOU.

HTTPS://YOUTU.BE/4AWKQE4O9KE

(TIP: WORDPRESS IS A WEBSITE WITH A BLOG. THIS IS GOOD FOR YOU BECAUSE YOU CAN MAKE YOUR WEBSITE MORE POPULAR WITH GOOGLE IF YOU WILL MAKE 1 OR 2 NEW POSTS EVERY ONCE IN A WHILE AND TALK ABOUT DOGS, OR KEEP A DIARY OF YOUR DAYS WITH THE DOGS

AND MAKE SURE TO INCLUDE WORDS LIKE DOGGY DAYCARE OR SITTING DOGS WILL MOVE YOU UP IN SEARCH RESULTS. THINK OF A BLOG AS A WAY TO SHARE PERSONAL INSIGHTS INTO YOUR DAILY BUSINESS WHILE GETTING FREE ADVERTISING.)

YOUR WEBSITE SHOULD CONTAIN A BASIC STATEMENT ON WHAT SERVICES YOU OFFER. IT CAN INCLUDE YOUR PRICE RATES, YOUR PHONE NUMBER, AND ANYTHING ELSE THAT WILL BE HELPFUL IN GETTING A POTENTIAL CUSTOMER INTERESTED IN WHAT YOU HAVE TO OFFER. YOU'RE LOOKING TO OFFER A SAFE AND CONVENIENT SERVICE TO DOG OWNERS WITH THE BASIC INFORMATION THAT ANY BUSINESS WOULD OFFER.

ACTION STEP: WATCH THE VIDEO LINK ABOVE AND SIGNUP AND BUILD YOUR WEBSITE WITH WORDPRESS RIGHT NOW. DON'T PUT IT OFF! DON'T MOVE TO CHAPTER 8 UNTIL YOU'VE DONE THIS!

8. A FLIER THAT "GETS" BUSINESS

A GOOD FLIER IS NOT A SALES PITCH. IT'S A QUICK AND CONVINCING MESSAGE THAT OFFERS BENEFITS TO THE VERY PEOPLE WHO NEED THEM. NO SELLING INVOLVED.

A GOOD FLIER FOR YOU IS GOING TO STATE YOUR MAIN FUNCTIONS AND BENEFITS. HERE'S A FLIER EXAMPLE FOR YOU:

LET US WATCH FIDO WHILE YOU'RE AWAY   (INCLUDE SOME PICTURES IN THIS

                                                  AREA   WITH   YOUR BUSINESS LOGO)

*DOG BOARDING/SITTING/ IN OUR HOME OR YOURS

*UPDATES AND PICS OF YOUR DOG SENT TO YOUR CELL PHONE SO YOU CAN STAY UP TO DATE WHILE YOU'RE TRAVELING OR ON VACATION

*A HEALTHY AND FUN DOG LOVING ENVIRONMENT- WE SCREEN FOR ONLY THE BEST BEHAVED AND FRIENDLIEST DOGS

^^CALL TODAY AND MENTION THIS FLIER FOR A FREE DAY/20% OFF ON US!

PHONE NUMBER | BUSINESS NAME | BUSINESS WEBSITE

FLIERS SHOULD CONTAIN A FEW PHOTOS OF HAPPY DOGS AND YOUR HOME, AND THE BOTTOM OF THE FLYER SHOULD HAVE YOUR PHONE NUMBER AND DOGGY DAYCARE WEBSITE/BUSINESS NAME IN EASY TO TEAR OFF STRIPS SO POTENTIAL CUSTOMERS CAN RIP OFF YOUR CONTACT INFO FROM THE FLIER WHILE LEAVING THE FLIER UP AND POSTED.

YOU'LL NOTICE THAT MY FLIER CONCEPT OFFERS THE MAIN DETAILS AND BENEFITS OF THE SERVICE, AS WELL AS A CALL TO ACTION AND AN EXCLUSIVE BENEFIT IF THEY ACT ON THE EXCLUSIVE INFO THEY HAVE JUST RECEIVED. ALSO, BY OFFERING A FREE DAY FOR THEM, YOU ARE DEMONSTRATING YOUR CONFIDENCE AS WELL AS MAKING YOUR SERVICE A RISK-FREE DECISION FOR THEM. YOU COULD ALSO SKIP THE FREE OFFER AND SAY 20% OFF INSTEAD.

ACTION STEP: ONCE YOU HAVE A FLIER, YOU SHOULD DISTRIBUTE IT:

*TO EVERY HOTEL/MOTEL MANAGER IN TOWN WHETHER THEY OFFER PET FRIENDLY ROOMS OR NOT. YOU CAN ALSO INCLUDE A COVER LETTER WITH YOUR FLIER EXPLAINING TO HOTEL MANAGERS THAT IF THEIR HOTEL DOES NOT OFFER PET FRIENDLY ROOMS, THAT THEY CAN ARRANGE FOR DOGGY DAYCARE WITH YOU FOR OUT OF TOWN GUESTS AND TRAVELERS WITH DOGS SO THAT THEY CAN STILL GET THE TRAVELER'S BUSINESS AND RENT THEM A ROOM

*POST A FLYER AT EVERY DOG PARK BULLETIN BOARD, AT COFFEE SHOPS IN WEALTHY PARTS OF TOWN TO INCLUDE RESIDENTIAL STARBUCKS AND STARBUCKS IN LOCATIONS NEAR WHITE COLLAR BUSINESSES, AT CHURCHES IF THEY WILL LET YOU AND ANYWHERE ELSE YOU COULD SEE YOUR IDEAL CUSTOMER COULD BECOME AWARE OF IT... THINK ABOUT WHERE THE YOUNG PROFESSIONAL CROWD LIVES AND WORKS TOO

THINK

YOU HAVE A BRAIN. YOU HAVE A MIND. THINK:

1. "**WHO** ARE THE PEOPLE WHO HAVE TO GO TO WORK AND LEAVE THEIR DOGS AT HOME DURING THE DAY?"

----> WHERE ARE THE YOUNG PROFESSIONALS EARNING GOOD SALARIES, POTENTIALLY WELL-OFF BUT DISABLED RETIREES, OR JUST AFFLUENT PEOPLE IN GENERAL, LIVING?

2. "**WHAT** BUSINESSES, SUCH AS HOTELS, ARE *LOSING BUSINESS* BECAUSE THEY CAN'T ACCEPT CUSTOMERS WITH PETS/DOGS?"

----> MOST HOTELS ARE *NOT* DOG-FRIENDLY. THIS MEANS SOME HOTELS/MOTELS ARE LOSING BUSINESS BECAUSE THEY CAN'T ACCOMMODATE CERTAIN GUESTS. ALSO, THE PRICE OF THE NIGHTLY DOG FEE FOR MOTELS/HOTELS THAT *DO* ALLOW DOGS IS OFTEN THE SAME PRICE AS GETTING A SITTER FOR THEIR DOG. THIS MEANS OPPORTUNITY FOR YOU, NOW GO TAKE A FLIER TO EVERY MOTEL AND HOTEL IN YOUR AREA/CITY WITH A SMILE AND SOME CONVERSATION TO LET THEM KNOW HOW YOU CAN HELP THEM OUT.

3.   "**WHERE** DO PEOPLE WITH DOGS GO (SUCH AS A DOG PARK) THAT THEY CAN SEE A FLIER OFFERING THEM SOME TIME OFF FROM THEIR DOG AND A LITTLE FREEDOM IN THEIR LIVES?"

-----> MOST DOG PARKS HAVE SOME TYPE OF BULLETIN BOARD. PUT UP A FEW FLIERS WITH TEAR-OFF PHONE NUMBER STRIPS ADVERTISING YOUR SERVICES TO SIT/WALK/BOARD THEIR DOGS SO THEY CAN HAVE SOME FREE TIME AWAY FROM FIDO. ALSO, YOU CAN GO DOOR-TO-DOOR IN NICE NEIGHBORHOODS AND HANG A CUTE, FUN FLIER UP ON THEIR DOORS LETTING THEM KNOW ABOUT YOUR DOG WALKING/SITTING SERVICES.

(I USED TO GO DOOR TO DOOR RAISING MONEY FOR AN ENVIRONMENTAL CAUSE, AND ONE TIME I RAN FOR OFFICE AND WENT DOOR TO DOOR HANGING UP FLIERS. IF I CAN DO IT, SO CAN YOU.)

4. **"WHY** WOULD ANYONE HELP OR RECOMMEND YOUR DOG SITTING, DOGGY DAYCARE BOARDING OR DOG WALKING BUSINESS ANYWAY?

------> OTHER DOG RELATED BUSINESSES TO INCLUDE IN YOUR FLIER DISTRIBUTION STRATEGY:

... all businesses that are frequented by dog owners, such as *groomers, kennels, pet stores, community animal shelters, and veterinarians.*

RELY ON *THEIR* LOVE OF DOGS WHEN YOU BUILD RAPPORT WITH THEM. TELL THEM WITH CHEER ABOUT YOUR DOG SITTING/WALKING BUSINESS AND THAT YOU'D BE HAPPY TO REFER YOUR CLIENTS TO THEM AS WELL. TAKE ONE OF THEIR BUSINESS CARDS AS YOU DROP OFF SOME FLIERS.

9. HOW TO CREATE A GOOGLE BUSINESS LISTING FOR YOUR BUSINESS

This step is a game changer. This is another step that Rover.com sitters do not do and I know that if you will do this step, you will be so far ahead of the game it wil be silly. So do this step. It's ridiculously easy and the benefits and results are almost unfair to the competition. Most businesses don't even take this seriously and they pay dearly for it.

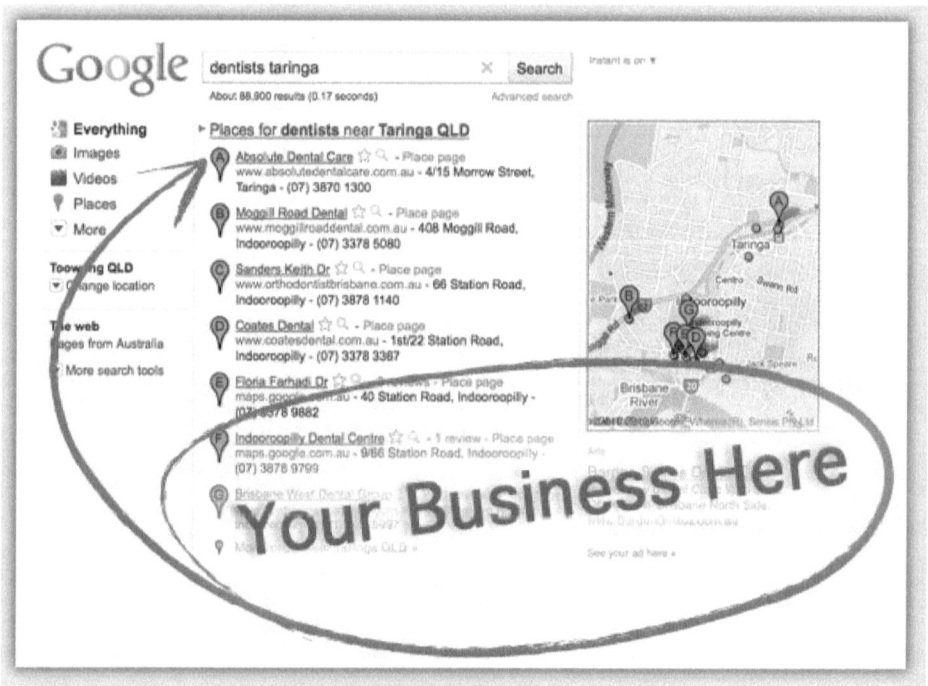

Having a strong internet presence just turned from nice to have optional addition to a mandatory requirement for almost all large, medium and small business. But at the same time, the internet has become incredibly competitive. So, how does a small pop and mom business stay afloat in the midst of the big boys without a big ad spend?

The answer is pretty simple; create a Google Local Business Listing.

And the best part is it's free, but it works so well you'd be willing to pay for it.

A Google Local Business Listing is basically a provision by Google for business owners to list their businesses in the local Google business database. Essentially, you provide accurate information to Google about your business, and this information is provided to people looking for what you have to offer, for free.

This shows up huge on both desktop and laptop computers as well as smart phones when people are rolling into town looking for a place to board their dog on their mobile device. See the advantage you will have with a simple website and link to your Google Business Listing? Simple but deadly effective.

These include your name, business name, address directions, category of business, and so on. This offering was launched early 2014, and it combines all the company's previous Google+, Google Local, Google Places into one platform. This is good news because it eliminates the hustle of keeping track of multiple accounts.

How to create a Google business listing for your business

It can get a little tricky with all the changes that have happened to Google's business listing offers –having ploughed through Google+, Google Local, Google Places and now Google My Business. But the good news is that Google's business listing cuts down the hustle of managing multiple accounts as it combines the advantages and functionalities of all the previous offers into one. So here are the steps you need to get your business listed on Google My Business.

a. Start by going to -http://google.com/places.

On the Google Places homepage, check the box that requests you to agree to the terms and conditions, and then click continue'.

b. Find your business or add it if it is not present.

Enter your business name in the search area and click on Search' to see if it is listed. If your business is listed, click on it and edit (proceed to step 7). If none of the business listed is yours, click on "No, these are not my businesses. Let me create my business." Proceed to step 3.

c. Add your business information.

Your business address, business name, and phone number should match exactly what you have o your website. Otherwise, Google may not know which details are correct, and this may greatly hurt your rankings. Also, they will want to send you a postcard with a code to activate the business, so the address has to be correct for you to receive the postcard for activation.

YOU MUST ENTER YOUR BUSINESS WEBSITE/URL IN THE SECTION WHERE IT IS ALLOWED TO HAVE MAXIMUM BENEFIT. DO NOT CONSIDER YOUR GOOGLE LISTING COMPLETE WITHOUT IT LINKING TO YOUR WEBSITE.

d. Select your business category(s).

The business category is considered the most critical ranking factor. Be very carefully and choose the correct category keeping in mind that the primary category is the most important. Choose the secondary categories basing your choice on what your business is, as opposed to what it does. Keep in mind that Google no longer accept categories that are not on their list.

e. Service Area.

If your business is strictly retail and does all its daily transactions at its store, click submit and proceed to step 6, otherwise click the box against "I deliver goods and services to my customers at their location." if you deliver services and products to your clients' locations. If you do, a new box will pop up with an option to specify your service area.

f. Verify your listing.

Google gives you an option to verify your business either by phone or regular mail. You can also choose to save and verify later. In my opinion, for obvious reasons, I would advise that you opt for phone verification.

Tips on how to optimizing your Google Business Page

· Business name: Use your real name and avoid adding location or keywords in order improve your rankings.

· Address: Your service area and address information will often populate automatically from your entries in step 3 and 5 above. You can however edit this by hovering over the items

· Contact info: Use your local business number, as for your website address, use the actual web page or website associated with your business. A Google business listing is worth its weight in gold for just this one link to your business URL and the boost it provides you.

· Photos: The old version only allowed up to a maximum of 10 photos, the current new version allows up to 20 photos. Choose the images that best represent your business. For maximizing your Google rank, rename all your pictures to keywords specific to your area before uploading the pics. Example: dog boarding Raleigh, doggy daycare Toledo, etc

Benefits of a Google Local Business Listing

· Help you reach millions of users quickly and free. One link from Google to your business URL is going to boost you way up in the search engines when people look for dog sitters

· Freedom to edit your listings and showcase the most important elements to you and your business.

· Practical and quite easy to use

· Premiums services available for free.

· Signup is simple and free.

· Improved search engine rankings

· Effective marketing and exposure of your business locally.

Action Step: Go create your Google Business Listing Right Now!

10. MAKE GOOGLE, FACEBOOK AND YOUTUBE WORK FOR YOU

FILMING SOME SIMPLE VIDEOS OF DOGS PLAYING THAT YOU WATCH AND TITLING THE VIDEO DOGGY DAYCARE IN <YOUR TOWN NAME> AND THEN

PUTTING YOU WEBSITE LINK HTTP://YOURSITE.COM IN THE INFORMATION/DESCRIPTION FIELD ALONG WITH YOUR BUSINESS ADDRESS AND PHONE NUMBER OF THE YOUTUBE VIDEO CAN SKYROCKET BOTH THE VIDEO AND YOUR WEBSITE TO THE TOP OF GOOGLE RANKINGS. THIS CAN LEAD TO MORE CLIENTS FOR YOU.

VIDEOS ON YOUTUBE OFTEN TIMES WILL SHOW UP IN THE TOP 10 SEARCH RESULTS ON GOOGLE, FOR FREE. SO TAKE GREAT CARE IN THE PRIOR MENTIONED INSTRUCTIONS ON HOW TO TITLE YOUR VIDEO AND TAG IT WITH VARIOUS IMPORTANT KEYWORDS, WHILE PUTTING YOUR ADDRESS WEBSITE AND PHONE INFO IN THE DESCRIPTION FIELD. I CAN'T STRESS THIS ENOUGH!

A SIMPLE PROMOTIONAL VIDEO CAN BE MADE BY FILMING SOME GREAT FOOTAGE OF THE DOGS YOU WATCH PLAYING, THEM SLEEPING, DOING CUTE THINGS, ETC. AND LINKING TO YOUR WEBSITE. SO IT'S GOOD TO TAKE VIDEO OF YOUR DOGGY CUSTOMERS AND COMPILE THESE VIDEOS, THEN PUT THEM TO SOME MUSIC AND UPLOAD THEM TO YOUTUBE. AGAIN, IF YOU DON'T KNOW HOW TO COMPILE VIDEO AND PUT IT TO MUSIC, HIRE SOMEONE FROM FIVER.COM FOR CHEAP TO DO IT FOR YOU.

DO NOT WASTE YOUR TIME ON FACEBOOK POSTING ENDLESSLY TO NO ONE WHO SEES IT. DO NOT WASTE YOUR TIME WITH TWITTER OR PINTEREST. YOUR BREAD AND BUTTER ARE ROVER.COM, GOOGLE, A FEW BLOG POSTS, A FEW FACEBOOK POSTS AND VIDEOS HERE AND THERE LINKING TO YOUR WEBSITE WITH GOOD TITLES THAT MAKE IT EASY FOR SEARCH ENGINES TO FIND YOU REGARDING DOG BOARDING, DAYCARE, SITTING AND WALKING, AND A SUPER TARGETED FLIER CAMPAIGN IN

YOUR AREA WITH OUTREACH TO HOTELS/MOTELS AND OTHER BUSINESSES THAT WOULD BENEFIT FROM OFFERING YOUR SERVICES.

A GOOD STRATEGY WITH FACEBOOK IS TO CREATE A BUSINESS PAGE FOR YOUR DOG SITTING/WALKING SERVICE, AND THEN TAKE A FEW PICTURES HERE AND THERE, AND POST THEM UP SO THAT YOU'LL HAVE ONE MORE ADDITIONAL SOURCE OF POSITIVE PUBLICITY FOR YOURSELF.

IT'S ALSO POSSIBLE FOR YOU TO TAKE PICTURES OF THE CLIENTS' DOGS AND THEN TAG THE PEOPLE ON FACEBOOK, AND WHO KNOWS, THEY MIGHT SHARE THAT POST WITH THEIR FRIENDS AND THEN YOU'LL GET EVEN MORE BUSINESS.

11. THE DO'S AND DON'TS OF CUSTOMER SERVICE FOR SMALL BUSINESSES

If you have just started your small business, how you establish the right customer service ethos may make or break your business. The quality of customer service that you provide is extremely important. If you make blunders, you are not likely to get a second chance since you have no brand name or reputation to fall back on, unlike the case for the larger and more established businesses.

To ensure that your business gets off on the right footing, you need to know the do's and don'ts of customer service as listed below:

Do:

1. Reply to emails/texts and return phone calls immediately. The customer should not be left hanging waiting for you to answer emails or calls.

2. Treat your customers with utmost respect and always appreciate them. Remember to say thank you when they make a payment, refer you to a potential customer or make a tweet about your services.

3. **Allow for payment with cash *and* credit card.** You can get a simple and easy credit card reader that attaches to your smartphone and allows customers to pay you easily without requiring cash transactions. The fees are minimal for the benefits and freedom plus customer satisfaction you will gain.

4. Practice flexibility when resolving customer complaints. For example do not respond to all complaints by always saying that 'this is our policy'. This is a sure way of losing customers. Don't pretend to be right if you're not.

5. Readily admit your mistake when problems arise. This will assist you to build customer rapport and loyalty.

6. Deliver on your promise or better still, over-deliver. Ensure that you do exactly what you say you will do. This will help to buildup confidence among your customers, and will make your brand grow stronger.

7. Ask to get further clarification from your customers when you are not sure about what they require. You can suggest that they provide additional details so that you can resolve their issue more effectively.

8. Use customer complaints as an opportunity for improvement and as a way of making a stronger connection with your customers. Evaluate the complaint and try to see what adjustments you can make so it does not recur. Reassure the customer and offer total support to the customer. But if they are still not satisfied, offer them a refund or replacement.

Don't:

I. Make false promises or lie to customers about your products and services. Ensure that your terms are clearly described in all areas of your business, for example on receipts and on the sales page. Don't talk a big game.

II. Demand or ask directly for a review of your business. The customer's life is not about you or building your business by asking them to help you. That's your job.

III. Expect the customer to understand your mistake or oversight in an area that you are expected to be more knowledgeable about, for instance making simple mistakes they interpret as major. Just understand that some people are not reasonable, move on, and get over it.

IV. Use systems, processes or the environment as an excuse when faced with customer complaints. For example saying that customer service will improve when you move to bigger premises will not resonate well with your customers. Instead, concentrate on addressing the root cause of the problem. Work on improving your systems and processes and managing your resources better.

V. Leave a problem unresolved because the tone of a customer has offended you or due to any other reason. Always ensure that you remain courteous, calm and professional and avoid being abusive when replying to emails.

VI.   Talk ill about the competition. This reflects badly on you and will ruin your reputation. Remember that your customers may probably be interacting with your competitors in some way.

Action Step: If you have not already, <u>signup with PayPal and get a credit card reader to accept payments in person</u> easily and impress all your customers too

ADDITIONAL WAYS TO MAKE YOUR CUSTOMERS/CLIENTS LOVE YOU

There are some great ideas to make your customers fall in love with you. Use these 2, but come up with some on your own as well!

1. For people who get several days of boarding with you or repeat customers, it can be handy to take a picture of their dog and then get it printed out, put the picture on a funny card that says "Wish You Were Here" or "Enjoying My Doggy Vacation" so the customers will both have a sweet memory and positive reinforcement of boarding with you while having free word of mouth advertising and showing that you go above and beyond in your customer experience.

Doing something cute like this for the client will make them do backflips over you. They'll put the card on their desk at work or their refrigerator and you'll be top of mind.

2. Send Daily Updates. Send your customers a text either through Rover.com or through their own cell number (if you are getting independent clients) once a day of a happy picture of their dog outside running in the yard, playing with some other dogs, or sleeping. This will make the customer feel at ease and happy knowing their dog is having a good, safe, and well cared for time. It will take the guilt away from them knowing that they got a sitter for their dog, and will make them look forward to your customer service! Trust me on this one.

Extra Information

No one said this was going to be completely easy or the most perfect way to make money. There are **good and bad reviews and opinions** regarding Rover.com or running a dog boarding business from home.

Sometimes, business can be feast or famine. This means sometimes you feel like you can't get any business, and some days you get 2 or 3 new clients. Life is pretty random and unpredictable this way. Your best bet is to maintain your own mental toughness and find a way to get a steady influx of customers, and take care of and build a solid, loyal customer base so the dogs and their owners already know you, and it will make your life that much easier and more profitable.

One Final Note of Encouragement: I have met people who did this full-time or in addition to their social security check. They really enjoyed it and made a decent living at it. The strategies in this guide are intended to give you the outlook and immediate opportunities, along with a long-term strategy, to have your very own successful dog sitting/walking business!

Real Reviews from Sitters on Rover.com (good and bad)

"Rover is an incredible platform! I'm in Nursing School and watching dogs on the side for extra cash. I can't even begin to say how much fun we've had and the awesome things we've been able to do with the dogs."

"Great environment for starting your own personal side business. You can make or break your own career. Its up to you to build your business!"

"I love spending time with dogs. It's nice that rover.com gives me the oportunity to this job disregarding my age."

"You pick your clients, so there are no mistakes about how many hours you get. You pick your rate, so there's no worry about not making enough money.

It is as-needed and you are your own boss. Rover simply provides a means for those in need of a dog sitter or walker to find you!

The hardest part of the job is not having anyone contact you, since it's as needed there's no guarantee you're working every day of the week. The most enjoyable part is definitely animals! You get to form a special bond with every animal you encounter when you work for Rover. That's something i've always loved."

"I have really enjoyed working with Rover to build my pet sitting business. I highly recommend Rover to anyone who has a kind heart, loves animals and wants to gain a great Business!"

"A typical day at work envolves me doing what I like to do best, working with animals and making sure they are always safe and secure."

Dog Sitter (Current Employee) – New York, NY – July 6, 2016

I am a Rover dog sitter and have been for about 5 years now. I love it for many reasons but the first one being a love dogs. I don't own my own so being able to have dogs in my life is a plus. Also, it is a great way to make side money. You make your own schedule and you can me as busy as you want to be. Its up to you. I highly recommend using Rover as a dog sitter. It's the best!"

"A typical day at work envolves me doing what I like to do best, working with animals and making sure they are always safe and secure."

"Rover.com has given me the freedom to start a business that I am truly passionate about. Their platform gives me the tools I need that, as a single employee, I would not have had the resources to purchase on my own. They give you marketing tools, and interactive calendar, complimentary insurance, and even a mobile app to message with dog owners & clients. Without this help, I could have never grown my client base to the size it is today. I love being able to choose my own schedule and set my own rates (especially during the busy holiday season!)."

There was little to gain working for Rover, customer service does not care about you and will be condescending in their correspondence. Despite, following their protocols my fees were deducted a substantial 80% from my earnings, leaving me with $10 for a week of dog sitting two stubborn Pomeranian dogs with limited manners and discipline. Not only that, you may have to deal with unreasonable, demanding pet parents with no manners, compassion or respect for your time, property or well-being. You as a sitter have to compete in a over-saturated market and have to set your rates low because everyone does it too. Despite, being told you have the opportunity and right to set your own rates, the free market dictates your fees, it's about supply and demand. In addition, as a sitter you are not expected to buy insurance, but have to anyway if you want to attract clients. Rover is a bait and switch game, one not worth playing.

I had the displeasure of having my legs scratch up, my floors being defecated on twice by a stubborn dog that refuses to relieve itself on walks and bathroom breaks. You will lose sleep, you will slave away and receive no compassion from Rover or the dog owners. I never received my payment in full for the work I did in good faith and Rover.com does not care. The insurance plan does not cover anything and you will not be reimburse for any damages done to property, or any bodily damages a dog inflicts on you, it comes out of your paycheck.

You can be compassionate and kind but that won't get you very far, you will only be taken advantage of.

Too much loss and nothing to gain from Rover. There is no way to screen out underwhelming pet owners as there is no rating system, often times you will end up in a situation with no means for mitigation, and if you get stuck with a narcissist, high maintenance owner you are at a loss.

Rover's management will ignore you and fail to pay your wages, they will erase your account immediately after you voice any grievances.

"Dog Sitter (Former Employee) – San Diego, CA – February 23, 2016

I would not sign up for the protection plan they offer for $49.95. It is absolutely useless. I have had a horrible experience with the site and getting the funds I am owed. Almost all the dogs I sat for are horribly behaved and don't have any manners. The owners are demanding and don't plan well. I've had three dogs come to stay and they ran out of food while visiting. The owners refused to reimburse me and the protection plan doesn't cover food. Nor does it cover the destruction the dogs have inflicted on my house. I will never use this company again and am done with pet sitting in my own home game. This has just been an awful experience all around."

My own gripes as a Rover.com customer. The big reason I wrote this guide "Move Over, Rover!" is because I see a huge opportunity in this market. I have taken my own dog to so many different sitters, daycares, Rover.com sitters- that I have seen the massive demand for this type of service. Don't listen to people who say the market is over saturated. These people are NOT advertising outside of Rover.com. They are dependent solely upon Rover.com and their imperfect model. Dumb.

They are at the mercy of Rover.com, just one single website. You are not. You are going to have Google advertising you for free after I show you how. You are going to have connections all over town to REAL human beings who NEED you, they just don't know it yet, but you're going to let them know, and they're going to understand why. You're going to have a few strategic fliers placed around town in key areas. And you're going to go door to door and drop off fliers in nice neighborhoods to, because you understand THIS IS THE FAST WAY TO MONEY.

So don't let any of the negative reviews hold you back from doing this. Learn from them. This is why I'm going to show you how to pick and choose your customers and how many dogs you want to watch so you avoid the stress.

Making money is not about making a total sacrifice. It's about you and the customer/client winning at the same time. You're helping each other. That means love, not suffering.

My other gripes with Rover.com. I strongly believe they censor some negative reviews to keep their website looking trustworthy. I think they censored one of my reviews before which is a disservice to consumers. Controlling information and censoring is almost always bad practice and bad karma.

Also their lawyers contacted me while writing this guide demanding I take their logo down from the cover of the guide, even though I explained how it would only make them more money and help them have better customer service.

So on top of controlling information, they're hawking the web for anyone talking about them, which kind of creeps me out. And getting letters from lawyers with threats and demands is not fun either, especially when you've written positive reviews and made videos that promote their service for free because you like to help consumers.

Additionally, Rover.com sends its lawyers to even the smallest towns and communities in the USA attempting to re write laws to prevent the little guy from having their own dog sitting business outside of their website and program. They are literally trying to put people out of business who are not hurting anyone, just so they can have a monopoly on the market!

This again is why you need to be independent of websites like facebook, yelp, and Rover.com. Because in the end, none of them can really be trusted.

Well, that's about it. You now have a major advantage over every Rover.com sitter out there. It's up to you to apply the info and make it work. I know Rover.com sitters who run their own separate home doggy day care business and don't do a fraction of what I recommend in this guide.

This guide is the shortcut to building your business fast and effectively. I wish you great success with your new enterprise. -Patrick